Introverts, Extroverts, Verbal Aggressiveness, and Non-Verbal Communication in Organizations

4 Topics in 1 Book

Louis Bevoc

Published by
NutriNiche System LLC

For information contact:
info@nutriniche.com

Louis Bevoc books…simple explanations of complex subjects

Introverts and Extroverts in Organizations
Understanding the Importance of Both Personality Types

Louis Bevoc

Published by
NutriNiche System LLC

For information contact:
info@nutriniche.com

Louis Bevoc books...simple explanations of complex subjects

Introduction

This book focuses on introverted and extroverted employees in workplaces. It examines the roles they play in organizations while analyzing their strengths and weaknesses. The text is written in a simple format that is easily understood by readers at all levels.

Now that you understand the basic scope of this book, let's start with introverts. The first section discusses the pros and cons of introvert employees in organizations.

Introverts

What defines an introvert? At first glance, this question might seem easy to answer. However, in reality, it is difficult to answer without an in-depth understanding of introverts...and most people do not have that understanding. In fact, introverts are usually misunderstood because they rarely speak what is on their minds or let go of their emotions.

Introverted people prefer spending time alone rather than socializing with others. This does not mean that they want to be alone all of the time...they simply enjoy spending time by themselves to think, work, or do things they enjoy. In this respect, introverts are the opposite of extroverts who enjoy being with others and expressing their thoughts verbally.

Contrary to popular belief, introverts are not always shy. They appear shy because they tend to listen more than talk, and they usually do not speak unless they think they have something important to contribute to the conversation. However, this quietness should not be confused with shyness. Shy people are afraid to speak, while many introverts simply choose not to speak.

This same thinking applies to employees in organizations. Introverted workers are not necessarily shy...they are simply focused on their job tasks and prefer to work independently. They will speak when they feel the need, but their spoken words are carefully selected.

Advantages and disadvantages

Introverted employees exist in workplaces all over the world. Like every other employee, they work toward accomplishing the goals and objectives of the organizations that employ them. However, introverted workers offer specific advantages and disadvantages when performing their jobs as indicated by the following:

Advantages

The following are areas where introverts do well:

Listening

Introverted employees are very good listeners because they do not spend much time speaking. They absorb what is being said to them rather than trying to talk over the person who is speaking. Because they listen, they are able to make informed decisions about work-related matters without "shooting from the hip."

In short, introverted workers are a benefit to organizations because they have the natural ability to listen. They lend credibility to the saying, "listening is more important than talking….and that is why we have two ears and only one mouth."

Empathizing

Since introverts are good listeners, they tend to be more empathetic than other employees. They hear the problems and concerns of their coworkers and react with compassion. In this regard, introverts often display high levels of emotional intelligence.

Along the same lines, employees feel comfortable speaking with introverted coworkers. Again, this is because introverts listen better and react empathetically. Their words are often limited, but they tend to say the rights things with those few words.

Thinking

Many people speak before they think about what they are going to say. In organizations, this can cause problems that are difficult to resolve. If customers or regulatory agencies are involved, the consequences can be severe….even to the point where sales are lost or businesses are shut down.

Introverts always think before they react verbally to situations. They analyze the facts and make informed decisions. This prevents many problems from occurring, and it saves managers from experiencing unnecessary pain and suffering. In short, too many employees speak before they think, but this is not true about those who are introverted.

Self-directing

Introverts are very self-directed employees. Their ability to complete tasks without the help of others creates independence that is not found in many other workers. This means that introverts need less direct supervision than other employees.

Introverts are also self-motivated. They do not need outside sources of inspiration to perform their jobs, and they experience success under a variety of different circumstances. In other words, introverts do not need external rewards to keep focused.

Disadvantages

The following are areas where introverts do not do well:

Socializing

This is probably the most noticeable problem with introverts. Socializing is not a job requirement…and it even tends to hinder many people from doing their jobs when it becomes excessive. However, socializing is a part of most organizations, and it helps employees establish relationships with each other lead to teamwork and higher productivity.

Introverted employees are not typically interested in socializing, and they would rather be alone with their thoughts. This can create discomfort for employees that like to get to know each other. They see introverts as outsiders who have not entered into the social circle with other workers. Consequently, the bonds that form through socializing are not developed, and this can hinder the working relationships necessary to accomplish goals and objectives.

Collaborating

Not surprisingly, introverted employees are not particularly interested in team projects. They prefer to work alone, and they are usually competent in doing so. However, teams are capable of coming up with solutions to problems that result from multiple minds working together. Different backgrounds, knowledge, and experience help make informed decisions that take a variety of factors into account.

Multiple minds are important for decision making, and that is why so many organizations implement the team concept. This is one area where introverted employees fall short of being the best that they can be in their jobs.

Communicating

This might be the most damaging problem with introverts. Misunderstanding is common because they do not make themselves clear with their words or actions. They simply remain silent, and coworkers do not know what they are thinking.

As most people are aware, misunderstanding in workplaces causes problems that compound over time. This is not good for the organization or the people in it, and it can result from introverted behavior.

Disagreeing

Introverts rarely disagree with coworkers by voicing their beliefs and opinions. At first glance, it might seem strange that this is a disadvantage. After all, disagreements cause arguments and sometimes result in bitterness or other negative feelings. However, without disagreement, organizations do not undergo change.

In short, employees need to disagree...and introverted employees typically often have no desire to do so. They keep their thoughts to themselves, and this prevents their thoughts from being discussed or analyzed by others in the workplace. This is not good for the growth of workers or the organizations that employ them.

Now you are aware of some advantages and disadvantages of introverted behavior in workplaces. This leads to a question. Are introverts really needed in organizations? The answer to this question is yes...and the reasoning behind it will be explained in the next section.

Reasons they are needed

Sometimes it appears as if workplaces are designed for extroverted employees. After all, people need to communicate and collaborate with each other...and outgoing individuals seem to do this best. They express themselves through words and actions, and sometimes those words and actions are exactly what it takes to accomplish objectives.

As some people might expect, extroverted workers are typically more important to workplaces. However, organizations also need introverts to function at peak efficiency. Reasons introverted employees are needed include the following:

Organization

Introverts' intense focus on their work allows them to concentrate on the subject matter and keep everything in its proper place. In other words, they are able to stay organized and have no problems finding anything related to their job tasks.

Organization is a critical aspect of job performance. When employees are organized, they also manage their time better. They do not repeat unnecessary steps or processes, spend time looking for missing information, or ask questions that have already been answered. In terms of organization, introverts are needed by organizations.

Discretion

Introverted employees do not ask a lot of questions, but the questions they do ask are important. They do not "mince words" or stray off topics...they simply analyze situations and ask pertinent questions that help them complete their assigned tasks.

Believe it or not, some introverts make great interviewers. They focus on applicants and the jobs they are applying for...and they ask useful, strategic, and relevant questions. Their attention to detail and caution about choosing words also eliminates the potential for asking questions that are invasive or could bring about a lawsuit. In this regard, they are of great value to organizations.

Perspective

Due to their ability to listen intently, introverts view problems from different angles. They think things through for logical analyses, and this allows them to offer different perspectives for solutions. Diverse problem solving is critical for organizational growth, and this makes introverted employees valuable to their employers.

Self-awareness

People who take the time to critique themselves often discover their strong points and weak points. In fact, after a detailed analysis, they sometimes see things in themselves that others do not.

Most employees are not aware of their strengths and weaknesses because they do not critique themselves in detail. They believe they know what they do well and not so well, and they do not take the time to examine those beliefs in detail. However, this cannot be said about introverted employees. They are very self-reflective, and they tend to understand their strong and weak points. This understanding results in fewer mistakes and illogical actions...and that is good for any organization.

Writing

This is probably the least well-known strength of introverts. Their lack of speaking often results in them being good writers. They might not express their thoughts very well verbally, but they do a nice job of putting them on paper.

Their writing skills can also be expanded to areas beyond the normal thought processes of their coworkers. They can put abstract ideas and concepts into writing...and this is something that few other employees are capable of doing.

In business, a wide variety of important tasks require above average writing skills. These tasks are handling effectively and efficiently by introverts, thereby indicating their value to organizations.

Time Management

Introverted employees have limited interest in socializing with coworkers. Instead, they prefer to be immersed in their thought processes to solve problems and complete tasks. Focusing on the task at hand means they do not waste as much time as most workers, and this increases their value to their employers.

Self-sufficiency

Introverted employees are not attention seekers. There are not interested in being popular, and that type of recognition does very little to improve their work performance. In fact, most introverts would prefer not to have attention drawn to them, and too much of it hinders their ability to perform their jobs at the highest levels.

Attention helps many employees feel good about their jobs, but it cannot be the sole source of motivation because it is rarely, if ever, constant. Introverted workers are able to motivate themselves without attention, and this makes them valuable assets to their employers.

Derogatory comments

This trait is very important to management of organizations. Introverts keep their thoughts to themselves. They have been accused of not sharing enough information with coworkers, but this lack of sharing is good when the information is negative. Organizations are never short of employees who want to say bad things about management, and they welcome introverts who prefer to deal with their negative thinking internally.

Not surprisingly, introverted employees also have very little interest in gossip or rumors. They find them to be a waste of time and effort, and they lead to problems. Since management goes to great lengths to prevent rumors and gossip, they appreciate workplace introverts.

Conflict

Conflict is not all bad. In fact, functional conflict is a good way to initiate change and establish differing viewpoints. Without it, organizations tend to remain stagnant. However, dysfunction conflict is not good because it leads to people focusing on position rather than principle…and it often results in personal attacks.

Introverts typically do not arouse the emotions of their coworkers, and this does wonders for preventing dysfunctional conflict. When employees are emotionally charged, they tend to say things that they do not really mean or might not be true. This can upset others in the workplace and lead to unnecessary conflict that does little to resolve the issue at hand and leads to other problems.

In short, introverts get along with their coworkers. They typically like the people they work with and are liked by those same people. This is beneficial for management in organizations because it creates harmony in the workplace.

Haste

One thing for certain about introverted people is the fact that they do not jump to conclusions. They avoid reacting on impulse, and this prevents hasty decisions from being made. Obviously, this is something that most leaders of organizations find valuable.

Boredom

Introverts have a unique ability to focus intently on their jobs. They avoid large amounts of interaction with their coworkers, and they actually enjoy working alone. In short, they are able to thrive by themselves, and this means they rarely get bored. This works well for management because introverts are low maintenance employees.

Deadlines

Introverts tend to take pride in their work. They complete the tasks they are assigned in a designated time frame without supervision looking over their shoulders. They understand work expectations and adhere to them. This means that they do not miss deadlines....which cannot be said for all employees.

Now you understand the usefulness of introverts in organizations. This usefulness goes beyond the everyday employee since it is also applicable to leadership positions. The next section discusses the areas where introverts are valuable as leaders.

Leadership capabilities

Many people think that extroverted personalities are required for leaders of organizations. After all, leaders need to motivate their employees to do their best while working toward achieving organizational goals and objectives. This thinking, however, is not applicable in every instance. In fact, many employees are more motivated and productive working for introverted leaders.

Introverted leadership is preferred over extroverted leadership when:

Subordinate voices are important

Organizations that want their employees to be heard are often better off with introverted leaders. Introverts listen to people, and introverted leaders listen to their employees.

Employee input is important for virtually every company to operate effectively and efficiently, but it is critical for companies that employ primarily skilled workers. Engineering firms, welding companies, law offices, and consulting businesses are examples of organizations that depend on input from employees.

Structure is important

Introverted leaders can bring structure to organizations because they know how to organize. Structure is critical for organizations because it helps employees understand their roles. They are fully aware of their responsibilities and who they report to in the hierarchy.

Structure also helps managers understand what is expected of their employees. They are cognizant of organizational goals and objectives, and this helps them evaluate their employees' performance fairly and provide honest feedback for improvement.

In short, structure improves organizational communication...and introverts prioritize that structure when they are in leadership positions.

Thinking outside the box is important

Decision making is very important for every leader. They need to make sound and justifiable decisions using input from their employees...but they also need to avoid being swayed by those employees for the wrong reasons. Sometimes leaders need to forgo the general consensus of employees to make decisions that are best for their organizations.

Psychologist Irving Janis established the term "Groupthink" in 1972 to describe a process in which groups make irrational decisions when members attempt to conform to what they believe to be the consensus of the group. The end result is the group ultimately agreeing on something that each member might normally view as unwise.

Groupthink can cause organizations to stagnate...and even shut down permanently. Introverts help prevent groupthink because they listen to others and offer solutions to problems with unique perspectives. This "outside the box" thinking is critical for organizational growth and prosperity, and it makes introverts valuable leaders.

Emotional intelligence is important

In regard to leadership, emotional intelligence is essentially a leader's ability to recognize the emotions of others and respond appropriately and empathetically. This concept has been promoted in the workplace since the late 1990s when people like psychologist Daniel Goleman brought the idea to fame. It shows how and why emotions are a critical part of the way people interact with each other...and work relationships are essentially human interaction within organizational structures.

Empathy and emotional control can be critical for a leader's success since they allow for a greater understanding of what is really happening, thereby making decision-making more rational. Introverts are naturally more controlling of their emotions because they think before they react. This also helps them respond appropriately to other employees' emotional workplace reactions.

Self-directed work is important

There is little doubt that introverts are the best types of employees for self-directed work. They know what it takes to accomplish tasks without the help of others, and this is beneficial to organizations that prefer low-maintenance employees. That being said, it is a natural progression for introverted employees to transition into leadership positions where self-directed work is a high-priority.

Now you understand some situations where introverts are the best choice for the leadership positions. Unfortunately, more times than not, introverts are passed over for the top jobs because they are not good at self-promoting. They do not receive the attention or accolades that separate them from other workers, and this leads to them being overlooked.

Extroverted employees are much better drawing attention to themselves. They make contacts with important people, make sure their accomplishments are known, and "toot their own horn" regularly. This is annoying to some employees, but it works well for advancement to higher positions.

The traits and features associated with extroverted employees are often the same traits and features that people associate with leadership. This is one of the reasons why extroverted people have the lion's share of leadership positions in organizations.

Future

How does the future look for introverted employees? The answer depends on the situation. Managers are slowly realizing that introverts offer a diverse range of benefits. However, they also have some drawbacks.

The following explores the future for workplace introverts from a positive and negative perspective:

Positive

- They do not need the social aspects of workplaces. They can work alone for long periods of time with limited human interaction. Organizations of the future will need to be lean to compete, and this will naturally reduce socializing within them.
- They work well on their own, and employees will always need to think and act independently. Great organizations are built with people who motivate themselves to perform without the constant need for praise and attention.
- They are not disruptive. In other words, they do not create drama or conflict in workplaces and are therefore low maintenance in terms of needing to be supervised.

Negative

- They do not do well in open floor plans. The distractions of an open office cause problems for introverts because they like to spend time alone to think. Unfortunately, open floor plans will be a common aspect of many organizations in the future.

- They do not do well in teams. Like it or not, teams are going to be part of the future in workplaces all over the world…and introverts will benefit the least from them.
- They refrain from arguing. Although this is good in many instances, constructive arguing can be beneficial because employees are allowed to express and defend viewpoints that allow for choosing the best possible options.

So, what does this mean? It means that introverts have a place in future workforces. They will be needed, but they also need to be understood for their shortcomings by those who are different. Organizational leadership has progressed quite well when it comes to understanding introverted employee behavior…but this progression can be enhanced and improved.

Now, let's move on to discuss the pros and cons of extroverted employees in organizations.

Extroverts

Extroverts are social people who prefer being with others rather than spending time alone. They are not opposed to doing some things alone, but they like the excitement that an outside environment provides.

In organizations, extroverted people tend to stand out among other employees. They form relationships with their coworkers and get to know many of them on a personal and professional level. These relationships (especially those with management) help extroverts stay abreast of company happenings and maintain their visibility for advancement.

Advantages and disadvantages

Like introverts, extroverts exist in organizations all over the world. However, extroverted employees are more common than introverted workers. This, along with the fact they enjoy drawing attention to themselves, makes them much more noticeable in workplaces.

Specific advantages of extroverted employees are as follows:

Advantages

The following are areas where extroverts do well:

Communicating

Extroverted workers are good at communicating their thoughts and ideas. They have no problem letting others know how they feel about situations and are generally well understood. This is advantageous because people are never left wondering where they stand on issues or what they think should be done.

Acting

Thinking is great...but thoughts need to transfer into actions or some things do not get accomplished. Extroverts are great about acting on their thoughts because they are action-oriented. This is good for organizations because procrastination is not a problem with extroverted employees.

Directing

Extroverts are vocal, and they are not afraid to delegate. They are good at explaining what needs to be done, and they utilize the people they have available for task completion. This frees them up to move on to other areas that require their attention.

Collaborating

Teamwork is important in most organizations, and extroverted employees excel in this area. They work well with others to complete projects and resolve problems. Extroverts are great at expressing themselves, and this works well when collaborating with others.

Disadvantages

The following are areas where extroverts do not do well:

Listening

Extorted employees are good at expressing their own thoughts and ideas, but sometimes they are so involved with doing this that they fail to hear what others are saying. In other words, they are too busy talking to listen...and that can cause problems in organizations.

Empathizing

Empathy is critical for any type of leader, but it is also important for workers at lower levels in the organization. Employees want coworkers to understand and sympathize with their personal and professional problems. However, some extroverts are so busy fulfilling their own agenda that they fail to express any type of compassion...and this makes them look uncaring and arrogant.

Thinking

Extroverted employees are great at taking action. However, this can work against them if they do not think enough about the situation before they act. They sometimes do or say the wrong things simply because they did not think about the potential outcomes beforehand. It can be difficult to take back words that have been spoken, and extroverts often find themselves in this type of dilemma.

Working alone

People need to work alone to accomplish certain work-related tasks. Since extroverts prefer the company of others, they sometimes find it difficult to achieve goals and objects by themselves. This is not good for organizations or employees who depend on extroverts to properly do their jobs.

Now you are aware of some advantages and disadvantages of extroverted employees in workplaces. Let's move on to the next section that discusses the reasons extroverts are needed in organizations.

Reasons they are needed

As noted earlier, workplaces are mostly designed for extroverted employees. People need to communicate and collaborate, and extroverts do this better than other employees. They share their thoughts and ideas with others, and their words and actions work well to accomplish organizational goals and objectives.

Some major reasons extroverts are needed include:

Problem resolution

Extroverted employees are assertive and responsive to their surroundings. They are good at resolving problems because they act rather than wait to see what transpires. This is good because many problems must be resolved before organizations can move forward. Some workers become part of the problem because they do not have answers, but this is typically not the case for extroverts.

Inspiration

Everyone employee needs inspiration at some point in their career, and extroverts do well providing that inspiration. Inspired employees work hard to complete job-related tasks, and this is beneficial for the accomplishment of workplace goals and objectives. In short, extroverts help their coworkers feel good about their jobs and the organizations that employ them.

Ideas

Many employees who have ideas keep them inside their heads. Their ideas might work, but they are never exposed to others because the employees fear they will be stolen or rejected. Extroverts do not keep their thoughts to themselves, so their ideas are rarely lost. They are vocal about their thinking, and this helps companies grow and change.

Speaking

Nothing is worse than a boring speaker. Time drags and retention of the material being covered is minimal. The audience ends up frustrated, and the goal of the speech is not accomplished. In short, the speech ends up being a waste of money and time.

Organizations need speakers because information needs to be shared with customers, suppliers, industry personnel, employees, regulatory agencies, and the public. Extroverts are the best speakers because they thrive on being the focal point, and they enjoy the interaction with their audiences. They are able to keep people's attention while conveying the required information. This is beneficial to the organizations that employ them and the people that are listening.

Meetings

Extroverted employees do well in meetings because they get to interact with others, and they are able to express their views on the topics being discussed. Of special interest is the fact that extroverts are good in meetings as leaders or participants. Please consider the following:

Leaders

As leaders, extroverts do well because they discuss everything on the agenda in a pre-designated amount of time. They energetically address matters one by one and thrive on responses from other employees. Their animation often entertains participants, leads to more intense interaction, and creates a better learning environment.

Participants

As participants, extroverts do well because they enjoy discussing matters that pertain to their jobs. They like giving their opinions and getting feedback from other group members. Some extroverts even take over leadership roles at meetings due to their high level of interest and willingness to participate.

Negotiation

It is a simple fact that negotiation is important for the vast majority of workplaces. Poor negotiations can be the downfall of organizations because valuable resources are lost. For this reason, it is important to bring the right employees to the negotiation table.

Extroverted employees are excellent negotiators for two reasons:

Their personalities make them likeable

Many people think negotiations are not about personal likes and dislikes. This might be true in some cases, but it is much better to be liked than disliked by the opposing party. Concessions have a much better chance of being given to likeable people than they are to unlikeable people. Opposing parties tend to like extroverts because they are naturally social...and this can work wonders at the negotiating table.

They are intent on reaching their goals

Extroverts are driven towards being successful. That being said, they want to achieve pre-established goals during negotiations....and they work hard to reach those goals. Rarely do extroverts "throw in the towel" and concede. Instead, they use their skills to negotiate the best deal possible for their organization.

Change implementation

As noted earlier in this section, ideas from extroverts help bring about change in companies. However, their role does not stop here. Extroverts are also good at seeing change through to its completion. They can implement change and get others to embrace it. This is critical for organizations because without change they will eventually cease to exist.

Sales

Good salespeople are often extroverts. This makes sense because extroverted individuals like people and enjoy socializing. That socializing often leads to the establishment of the working relationships necessary for selling products or services. In short, organizations that want their products or services well-represented benefit from salespeople with extroverted personalities.

Public promotion

Extroverts represent their employers well using words and actions. They are able to present a positive image while appearing to have nothing to hide. That appearance is valuable for organizations that work with the public because it establishes trust....and trust is critical for public acceptance. Public relations nightmares are something that every organization wants to avoid, and extroverts often help prevent them from occurring.

Industry presence

Extroverts represent their organizations well in their designated industries because they have established friendships with a wide variety of people in those industries. In addition to knowing their customers and suppliers, they befriend individuals on important boards and committees...and they understand how to make themselves and their employers stand out from the competition. In terms of industry presence, extroverts are a valuable asset.

Government liaison

People in industries with limited government intervention typically do not know how good they have it. Government agencies, including the Environmental Protection Agency (EPA), Equal Employment Opportunity Commission (EEOC), Federal Aviation Administration (FAA), Federal Communications Commission (FCC), Food and Drug Administration (FDA), National Labor Relations Board (NLRB), Occupational Safety and Health Administration (OSHA), and Securities and Exchange Commission (SEC), can wreak havoc on organizations. They even have the power to prevent companies from doing certain types of business or operating at all.

Extroverts do well working with government agencies to help avoid the problems that those agencies can create. They keep everything out in the open and prevent government personnel from becoming upset over miscommunication or lack of information. The importance of extroverts in these types of situations is often overlooked...until it is too late.

Communication

This is likely the most obvious reason that extroverts are needed in organizations. They know how to communicate with others, and that is a skill that many other employees do not possess.

One particularly important area for utilizing communication skills is management-employee relations. Employees are not happy when they are under-informed or experience miscommunication, and extroverts do a good job preventing both of these from occurring. This saves management time, money, and the headaches that result from unhappy workers.

As you can see, extroverts are needed in organizations. Additionally, it is a known fact that they make good leaders. That being said, their leadership potential is discussed in the next section.

Leadership capabilities

Extroverted people make excellent leaders in a wide variety of organizations because they are assertive, outspoken, and motivational. Many employees like leaders who take charge, make decisions, and communicate organizational goals...and extroverts are capable of doing all of this and more.

Extroverted leadership is preferred when:

Direction is important

Extroverted leaders are exceptional delegators. Their outspoken and assertive personalities work well for issuing directions to employees to accomplish job-related tasks. This is good because leaders are able to move on to other areas of the workplace where they are needed. More specifically, it allows them to oversee the entire organization to make sure goals and objectives are achieved...rather than focusing on one specific task.

Collaboration is important

Teams are a big part of many organizations today, and they require people working together to resolve issues, finish projects, or complete tasks. Extroverts know how to work with others and accomplish goals. They excel during interaction and feed off the comments of other employees. They are natural group leaders because they are in an environment that allows them to reach their maximum potential. They are by far the best leaders for organizations that require large amounts of collaboration.

Reaction is important

Some workplaces need decisions made sooner rather than later because they lose out if they wait too long. An example is a brokerage firm that day trades stocks. Managers need to make fast decisions that can make or break their customers. Extroverts do not sit back and wait to see what happens. Instead, they react...and this makes them well-suited for organizations that need quick responses to situations.

Change is important

As noted earlier, extroverts do well with change. They can implement it and get people to accept it. This is a skill that few people possess, and it is important because all workplaces go through change at some point. However, some organizations experience more change than others, and those organizations are better off with extroverted leaders.

Stimulation is important

This might be the biggest strength of extroverted leaders. They can stimulate employees in the workforce so they perform their jobs at optimum levels. Without some type of stimulation, workers lose motivation. Ultimately, work becomes mundane, and performance levels drop. This is not good...especially in organizations that sell or market goods or services. These organizations need upbeat and outgoing leaders to be the best they can be...and extroverts fill that need very effectively.

Future

Extroverts will have a lot of positive offerings for workplaces in the future. However, these offerings will also come with some drawbacks.

The following explores the future for workplace extroverts from a positive and negative perspective:

Positive

- They work well with a wide variety of people and personalities. They thrive on interaction, and socializing is natural to them. This will be beneficial in the future as organizations become more global and cultures merge. Employees will need to work with individuals who are different, and extroverts will lead the way.
- They motivate employees, and there will always be a need for motivation in workplaces. This motivation can also be applied to team situations...and teams are going to be a part of workplaces everywhere.
- They inspire change. Believe it or not, this might be the biggest positive of extroverts in the future. Change is critical for the survival of organizations, and it helps them grow and prosper. In short, change was essential in the past, it is essential now, and it will be essential in the future.

Negative

- They do not do well independently because they need external stimuli for motivation. Certain job tasks are best performed alone, and extroverts are not the best choice for those jobs.
- They often form shallow or superficial relationships that mean relatively nothing. Their constant need for engagement means that quality time cannot be spent with every person they meet...and consequently some people get pushed to the back burner in terms of friendship. This makes extroverts appear insincere or uncaring.
- They cause conflict. Conflict can be good if it is functional, but dysfunctional conflict causes a variety of problems. Some employees find extroverts to be annoying or bothersome, and this can result in dysfunction conflict that turns into personal attacks.

So, what does this mean? It means that extroverts will be valuable as employees and leaders in the future. They will be essential for helping organizations change and progress, but they need to be aware that they can cause workplace problems in terms of conflict or appearing arrogant. Extroverts are a big part of workplaces today, and this will not change in the future.

Summary

Introverted and extroverted employees exist in workplaces all over the world. They are different in terms of the ways they approach their jobs, but they have a common goal of accomplishing organizational objectives. Neither personality type is going to disappear, so a better understanding of each is important to everyone in the workforce.

This book focuses on introverts and extroverts in organizations. It discusses their strengths, weaknesses, and capacity to assume leadership roles. It is educational and informational, and the text is written so that it is easily understood by readers at all levels.

Congratulations! You now understand more about workplace introverts and extroverts....many of whom play important roles in organizations all over the world.

Verbal Aggressiveness in Organizations

Understanding and Exemplifying

Louis Bevoc

Published by
NutriNiche System LLC

For information contact:
info@nutriniche.com

Louis Bevoc books...simple explanations of complex subjects

Introduction

In the mid-1980s, Dominic Infante and C.J. Wigley defined verbal aggressiveness as a destructive form of communication involving an attack on the personal beliefs or self-concepts of others. At the time, that definition was based mostly on studies involving interpersonal relationships. Today, it can be applied to workplace relationships.

Unfortunately, verbal aggressiveness occurs in workplaces all over the world. The type of organization or industry sometimes plays a role in the amount that occurs, but it is virtually impossible to find a workplace where employees have never experienced any type of verbally aggressive behavior by their coworkers.

Employees use verbal aggressiveness for many reasons including lack of argumentative skills, trying to be humorous, being mad or in a bad mood, trying to appear "tough," and compliance gaining purposes. Regardless of the reason, these attacks send a negative message and the effects are rarely positive.

Each of these reasons is examined in more details as follows:

Lack of argumentative skills

Contrary to what some people believe, arguing has some benefits. It allows people to express their viewpoints and hear the viewpoints of others. People who can "swallow their pride" can learn a lot from arguing, and they can apply that knowledge to future situations for constructive resolution of problems.

Swallowing one's pride, however, is often easier said than done....and this is why many people have difficulty arguing. The emotions they experience during arguments make them feel uncomfortable, and they have difficulty expressing their viewpoints without fumbling for words. They say things that they do not really mean...and they end up appearing under-informed or clueless while defending their positions.

Employees who have difficulty arguing sometimes resort to alternative methods for getting their point across. They raise their voice because they believe this strengthens their position, or they walk away indicating that their opponent is not worthy of their time. These methods do little to resolve the actual problem, and they typically are not effective.

A far worse combat strategy used by employees who lack arguing skills involves personally attacking their opponents. They mock people's physical appearance, past accomplishments, thoughts, beliefs, or ideas. This does nothing for defending positions, and it is offensive to the people who are being attacked.

Organizational example

Travis is a production supervisor at a brewery. He has been with the company for nine years, with the last three being spent in his current position.

One of Travis' bottling lines is stopped by the quality assurance manager Janice because the beer that does not meet the company requirement for color. This upsets Travis, and he tells Janice that her action is not justified. Janice calmly explains that the color of the beer is not right, and the line can be restarted after this issue is corrected. Travis believes the color is acceptable, and he becomes irate.

Rather than involving herself in a heated argument, Janice says she will get the color speciation chart from the laboratory to support her action. Instead of arguing his position on the matter, Travis tells Janice that quality assurance personnel are a total waste of money. He says that they work against the best interests of the company, and their department should be eliminated.

Without saying a word, Janice walks away and gets the plant manager so he can decide on the color of the beer. The plant manager supports Janice, and the line is stopped until the color of the beer complies with company specifications.

In this situation, Travis attacked Janice and her department because he did not have a legitimate argument for his belief that beer was the right color. Ultimately, his action created a relationship issue between himself and Janice, and it did nothing to defend his position.

Trying to be humorous

Unfortunately, some people think it is funny when they attack others personally. In workplaces, employees who attack other employees often have an audience of coworkers present that they believe are being "entertained." People witnessing the verbally aggressive behavior might laugh, but usually, this is because they are uncomfortable. However, people being targeted by the verbal aggressiveness find absolutely no humor in the situation.

Organizational example

Serena is the paint department manager at a retail superstore. She employs five high school students in her department, and she makes it a point to make fun of them in front of other employees. She jokes about them being kids and their inability to perform simple job tasks without direct supervision.

Some of Serena's coworkers laugh at her comments, but this is mainly because they feel uncomfortable. They like the high school students and believe they are trying their best to do their jobs...but they also want to show that they have a sense of humor.

The high school students, however, do not find Serena's derogatory comments funny at all. They might not be seasoned employees, but they are not children, and they believe they are capable of completing tasks on their own.

Ultimately, Serena's verbal aggressiveness has a negative impact on the employees in the organization. She believes she is entertaining coworkers with her humor, when in fact she is offending some of them and creating discomfort for others.

Being mad or in a bad mood

Everyone experiences bad moods. This is completely normal because things do not always go as people hope or plan, and negative emotions can surface. Unfortunately, those negative emotions can build in people to the point where they react in some type of hostile manner...including verbally attacking others.

Employees who are in bad moods sometimes take out their frustration on their coworkers by saying hurtful things that inflict psychological pain. This is bad because people say things that they do not really mean...but the damage is done, and it is difficult to reverse.

Organizational example

Jeremy is a construction supervisor. He and his wife always eat breakfast together before they both go to work. This morning, however, they get into an argument over finances at the breakfast table. Jeremy believes his wife spends too much money on unnecessary things, and she disagrees with him.

Jeremy shows up for work in a bad mood due to the argument with his spouse. At the first job he visits, he finds that his employees have made a mistake on the driveway they are pouring for a customer. They mistakenly poured five inches of cement instead of the agreed-upon four inches, and this means the job will not be profitable.

Jeremy is angry about this mistake, and he starts yelling at his employees. He calls them stupid and incompetent and tells them they should all be fired for making such a dumb mistake. The workers are demoralized and begrudgingly go back to doing their jobs.

Jeremy has been in the construction business for over 20 years, and he has seen this same mistake made in the past. He knows that this job will not be profitable, but it will not lose money for the company. His verbal aggressiveness resulted from the bad mood he was in due to the confrontation he had with his wife. Unfortunately, his words demotivated his employees and damaged his relationship with them.

Trying to appear "tough"

Some employees think that their verbal aggressiveness makes them appear stronger or tougher than others. They believe their language will prevent others from taking advantage of them or "stepping on their turf."

Employees who implement verbally aggressive strategies for toughness have thought about the psychological harm they are doing to others. This differs from being mad or in a bad mood because the hurt is intended and those inflicting the pain really do mean what they say.

Organizational example

Albert is a welder at a metal fabrication shop. He likes to do stainless steel welding, and he does everything in his power to make sure he gets assigned to the stainless jobs without the help of any other employees.

One of Albert's ways to prevent other employees from working on stainless steel projects is to attack their ability to do the job. Stainless steel welding requires special skills, and Albert has those skills. Other employees also have the skills, but they are not as talented as Albert...and he makes sure he lets them know it.

Albert makes fun of the other employees by laughing at the jobs they have completed. He tells them that they do not have the knowledge or skills to be stainless steel welders, and they should stick to the easier jobs to avoid getting fired for incompetence.

Albert's verbal aggressiveness results from him wanting to appear "tough." He likes doing stainless steel welding, and he wants everyone else to stay away from any projects involving it...so he attacks his coworker's ability to properly perform their jobs.

Compliance gaining purposes

Compliance gaining occurs when employees attempt to get coworkers to comply with their desires, wishes, or demands. Skillful employees do this using tactfulness and diplomacy. However, workers who are unable or unwilling to be tactful or diplomatic, often resort to verbally aggressive language to gain compliance.

Threats are a form of verbal aggressiveness used for compliance gaining purposes. Specifically, employees threaten coworkers to control them...with the fear of consequences for not meeting demands.

Threats have successfully changed employees' behavior in some instances, but other times they simply do not work. This is because threats are only successful if the worker making the threat is willing to follow through if demands are not met. If the threatening person is tested and fails to follow through, then the threat was unsuccessful.

Unfortunately, some people never test out the willingness of another employee to follow through on a threat...and this causes them to live under the control of that employee. Older employees, for example, often "bluff" younger employees into performing their job function in a certain manner based on the threat that failure to do so will result in disciplinary action. The younger employees never think to question the older employees because of their experience, so the bluff works well.

However, this bluff is only successful as long as the younger employees continue to believe it is true. If they find it to be false, the result may be a verbally aggressive conflict due to the feelings of victimization by the younger employee. If this is the case, then verbally aggressive behavior (the threat of consequences) leads to more verbally aggressive behavior...and the end result is a dysfunctional organization.

Organizational example

Claudia is a nurse at a hospital. She works in the Intensive Care Unit, and she does not like other nurses to make any changes to her patients' care requirements without first getting her approval.

To accomplish her objective, Claudia threatens the other nurses. She tells them that any nurse who makes changes to her patients'care will be disciplined by the head nurse. She states that the head nurse only allows doctors and Claudia to makes changes to her patients' care.

In reality, Claudia's threat is not true. Other nurses will not be disciplined for making changes to her patients care requirements as long as they follow proper hospital protocol. However, Claudia's bluff works because none of the other nurses call her out on it. In other words, her threat is successful for compliance-gaining purposes.

Now that you understand some of the reasons that employees use verbal aggressiveness, let's move on to some less obvious ways that it occurs.

Boundaries

This encompasses the area or space in which verbal aggression can occur. Specifically, boundaries refer to the means or type of communication where the destructive messages can take place.

Channels

Some people believe that verbal aggressiveness only occurs during face-to-face interaction, but this is not true. Destructive messages can be delivered through a variety of other means. Telephones, fax machines, and computer devices are all mediums available for personal attacks. In fact, computer-mediated communication such as email, tweeting, and texting often leads to more frequent and deeper verbal aggressiveness than face-to-face communication. Since electronic mail remains in computer memory until deleted, people can reexamine messages to determine their exact meaning. Rereading verbally aggressive messages can be especially detrimental because the damage to self-concept is brought back in full force every time the destructive writing is viewed. The time needed for psychological healing is extended due to the visible reminder.

The point here is that people on the receiving end of a negative computer-mediated message are as likely to be offended as those in face-to-face discussions.

Organizational example

Henry is a design engineer who works at a computer software company. His job affords him the luxury of working full time out of his home office. For the most part, this works out very well for Henry. However, it does present an opportunity for communication problems.

Henry is working on a project with three other employees who work at the physical office. They email back and forth to exchange ideas and information, but sometimes it is hard to understand the true meaning of the messages being sent.

While corresponding with each other on the project, Henry sends out an email with some mild sarcasm that is intended to be humorous and harmless…but one of the other employees is offended by it. This creates unnecessary stress in the group, and productivity abruptly halts until it is resolved with a series of other emails.

Henry was not intending to assault or offend anyone working on the project, but another employee's perception of his sense of humor caused it to happen. In this case, the channel of communication caused an employee to view Henry's comments as verbally aggressive.

Non-verbal

It might seem surprising, but verbal aggressiveness is possible without saying a word. This is because people's actions affect the mental well-being of others. Silence, rolling one's eyes, or "flipping someone off" are all examples of behavior that is meant to assault the target's mental well-being.

This type of behavior in workplaces can have a major impact based on the relationships that people need to form to accomplish tasks.

Organizational example

Thomas is a salesperson at a company that sells women's makeup internationally. He attends a business meeting in Japan with a Japanese executive from a cosmetics distribution company.

At the start of the meeting, the executive hands Thomas his business card. Thomas puts the card in his shirt pocket. Without realizing it, Thomas insulted the Japanese executive because Japanese businesspeople place high importance on business cards. The cards are to be treated with respect, and part of that respect means carrying them in a proper case. Disrespecting the card is seen as disrespecting the person whose name is on it.

Thomas was unintentionally offensive due to cultural misunderstanding. However, regardless of the reason, his non-verbal actions were viewed as verbally aggressive.

Now you understand the reasons for workplace verbal aggressiveness and the fact that is not limited to verbal discussion or face-to-face interaction. Based on this understanding, let's move into an analysis of the effects that it has on employees.

Effects

Verbal aggressiveness can be very damaging. In fact, the psychological hurt that it produces can sometimes be more devastating than physical pain. For example, a punch that blackens a child's eye could ultimately result in less pain than that caused by the teasing of other children for being a "sissy" or "wimp." Also, psychological damage is not always healed as easily as physical injury.

In workplaces, verbal aggressiveness has many different negative effects. It is related to several factors including trust, motivation, job satisfaction, productivity, communication, absenteeism, and turnover.

The following examines the relationship of verbal aggressiveness and these factors:

Trust

As many people are aware, trust-building is a challenging endeavor. It takes time and effort to build the relationships necessary to establish trust, and that trust can be broken with a single action. The worst part about this is the fact that trust is difficult to restore once it is lost.

Trust building for organizations is no different than it is for people in their personal lives. Employees work with each other to establish relationships...and eventually, those relationships build trust. However, verbal aggressiveness can destroy those relationships or prevent them from being built.

Consider the following two trust-related factors and their relationship to verbal aggressiveness:

Fairness

If employees do not believe they are being treated fairly, then they lose trust in those who are treating them unfairly. They need trust because they are dependent on their organization to earn a living. They spend a good portion of their waking life at their place of employment, and they need to believe they are being treated fairly.

When employees are assaulted verbally, they do not believe they are being treated fairly. They lose trust in the people who are attacking them...and they also lose trust in the management personnel who let it happen.

Respect

In terms of building trust, respect is in a category by itself. It is not always perceived as important, but anyone who has attempted to build trust without respect knows that this perception is far from reality.

Verbal aggressiveness is very disrespectful because people are personally attacked. Those being assaulted lose respect for those assaulting them, and they also lose trust in management.

Motivation

Employees who experience delight, pride, and satisfaction are highly motivated. They naturally influence others in ways that promote harmony and teamwork in the workplace. Their radiance tends to be contagious...and this is good for organizations.

Verbal aggressiveness destroys positive feelings and leads to lower motivation. Harmony and teamwork take a backseat to fear and resentment, and teamwork is lost in the process. Unfortunately, negativity is also contagious...and this is not good for organizations.

Job satisfaction

In simple terms, this is the amount of satisfaction that employees derive from their jobs. Satisfied employees are involved with their organization, and they identify with its values. In other words, they are committed to their organization through psychological attachment.

Verbal aggressiveness impedes or destroys employees' psychological attachment to their workplaces. It prevents organizational goals and objectives from being achieved because workers lack the drive or desire to follow through.

In short, employees who experience job satisfaction are more committed because they are happier with their work environment. Verbal aggressiveness hinders job satisfaction, thereby lowering the commitment necessary for organizational growth and prosperity.

Productivity

Productivity is one of the most important aspects of an organization. If people do not perform their jobs effectively and efficiently, then the organization might cease to exist. Positive emotions, such as excitement and happiness, are catalysts for productivity. Negative emotions, such as anxiety and anger, make people less productive.

Verbal aggressiveness creates negative emotions and erodes productivity. People are less efficient and effective because they have been personally attacked. Happy employees work harder than unhappy ones...and people who have their mental well-being assaulted are unhappy.

Communication

Communication is the process of using words or behavior to express thoughts or exchange information. Organizational communication is needed for employees to complete tasks and accomplish goals, and this is achieved by working together and sharing information.

Communication is probably the most obvious factor affected by verbal aggressiveness. It is necessary for sending messages that carry meaning and convey information. When people are personally attacked, they tend to communicate less...and workplaces suffer because meaning and information are lost.

Absenteeism

It is rather obvious that absenteeism impacts the bottom lines of organizations. This impact is never good, and it can lead to some companies permanently shutting down.

The following are some important aspects of workplaces affected by absenteeism:

Efficiency

Absenteeism results in decreased efficiency. This is because experienced employees are missing from the workplace, and coworkers who are less familiar with their jobs need to fill in.

Morale

When employees are forced to take on additional work due to absenteeism, they often become frustrated with their jobs. They resent management for the increased workload, and their morale decreases.

Stress

When employees are forced to take on more work due to absenteeism, they experience job stress. Over time, this causes them to burnout...and that burnout causes their absenteeism to increase. It is rather ironic, but absenteeism results in absenteeism.

Verbal aggressiveness increases absenteeism because employees are left feeling despondent about their jobs. They wake up in the morning and have no desire to show up for work, so they call in absent. This hurts employees and employers...and it can snowball if nothing is done to stop the personal attacks that are occurring.

Turnover

When employees are subjected to verbal aggressiveness, they start to dislike their jobs. This causes them to leave their organizations for other positions.

A transient workforce is a problem because it results in repeated training and quality issues. This adds stress for managers and causes mistakes since new employees are unsure of how to properly complete tasks.

Organizations need to understand the effects of verbal aggressiveness to reduce employee turnover. Managers who prevent these types of personal attacks are investing in the long-term survival of their organizations.

Based on the above, it appears that all the effects of verbal aggressiveness are negative. However, this is not always the case...and the exceptions are explored in the next section.

Exceptions

Despite all of the findings concerning the negativity of verbal aggressiveness, it cannot always be assumed that the consequences will always be bad. Threats, for example, are not all harmful. The participants in the conflict and their relationship with each other do not necessarily have to be damaged.

One productive use of threats is for employees to let others know that they feel strongly about their positions and are committed to reaching their goals. People who risk negativity impacting the harmony of a workplace by using threats show others that they are serious about their stance on certain matters.

Another constructive use of verbal aggressiveness involves the military. In the military, it is accepted to publicly berate a member in order to achieve what is perceived as positive behavioral change. A boot camp drill sergeant, for example, might scream at a new recruit and call him or her derogatory names because her or his bed was not made properly. This type of verbal abuse would probably not be accepted if a hotel manager were to reprimand a maid similarly for the same infraction.

Sports also allow the use of verbal aggression. The hope is that the offended person will become angry and, ultimately, more physically aggressive. An example includes a football player who misses a tackle and is told by his coach that he is "weak" and "soft." The coach wants the player to become more combative by making him feel ashamed of his actions. This type of aggressive behavior would probably not be accepted if a store manager were to verbally abuse a stock person in the same manner for not being physically able to do a heavy lifting job.

Verbal aggressiveness has achieved positive results in organizations such as athletics and the military because competitive situations or behavioral change motivation justify its use. It works as a compliance gaining strategy in these instances because established practices within the cultures allow for the verbally aggressive acts to be conducted.

Summary

Verbal aggressiveness involves attacking others with words or actions. It is a personal or psychological assault on the mental well-being of others during some type of interaction. It goes on all over the world, and it is not limited to personal interaction.

This book examines verbal aggressiveness in organizations. It looks at the reasons employees use verbal aggression, the ways that it occurs in workplaces, and the effects it has on the workers it is directed toward.

Congratulations! You now understand more about workplace verbal aggressiveness...an important aspect of organizational behavior.

Non-Verbal Communication in Organizations

Understanding and Improving

Louis Bevoc

Published by
NutriNiche System LLC

For information contact:
info@nutriniche.com

Louis Bevoc books...simple explanations of complex subjects

Introduction

Communication is absolutely necessary for conveying information. Without it, the world would consist of people who lack synergy, cohesiveness, and understanding. This is why communication is so heavily researched in academia and workplaces.

Essentially, communication has three major categories. Let's define those categories from an organizational perspective:

Verbal communication

This is likely the most well-known form of communication. It is a major constituent of every organization, and it consists of the spoken word. Organizations establish norms regarding verbal communication that are followed by all employees. Factors such as culture, age, workplace terminology, and industry-specific jargon influence the way employees speak customers, suppliers, and coworkers.

Written communication

Written communication uses words in a variety of documents including letters, memos, reports, instructions, legal documents, and signs. The information can be handwritten, typed, or professionally developed, and it can be composed using word processors, computers, email, texting, tweeting, or instant messaging. Regardless of the method used to display the wording, written communication transfers information to others in writing.

Non-verbal communication

This involves just about every aspect of communication that is not spoken or written. Body and facial movements, gestures, expressions, positions, and appearance are all part of non-verbal communication. Voice tone, pitch, and quality also fall into this category because they are not spoken words.

The focus of this book is on non-verbal communication. More specifically, it examines the importance and effects of this type of communication in organizations using thoughtful analysis and employee examples. That being said, let's get started.

In general

People might not realize it, but a sizeable portion of their communication with others is non-verbal. Eye movement, posture, body position, hairstyle, body art, clothing, facial expression, shoulder shrugs, and hand gestures are all examples of non-verbal communication used to transfer information to others.

Certain elements of speech also play a role in non-verbal communication. These elements make up what is known as paralanguage, and they include voice quality, speed, pitch, tone, and volume. Paralanguage is so important that people even use it during written communication. For example, the use of capital letters in email effectively means the sender is yelling or trying to get the reader's attention.

Not surprisingly, non-verbal communication has a major bearing on organizations and the people within them. Employees communicate with coworkers, suppliers, customers, and others using a variety of different techniques that do not involve the spoken or written word. Something as simple as a handshake means has a meaning that is understood by the parties engaging in the activity. This behavior is quite common and typically friendly, but other employee actions are not as welcoming. Ignoring someone, for example, is a much more unfriendly type of behavior that also does not involve the spoken or written word...but it still has meaning for the people involved. In short, non-verbal communication influences employees' perceptions of others and affects their relationships.

An entire book could be devoted to defining non-verbal communication, but this book focuses on its influence on and involvement in organizational behavior. The above description gives you a basic understanding of the significance of non-verbal communication in organizations, so let's move into specific types that occur regularly.

Types

Non-verbal communication needs to be categorized for a better understanding of its relationship with workplace behavior. The following are specific types of non-verbal communication that occur in organizations:

Symbols

These are intentional gestures, movements, or motions by people to send signals or signs to others. Waving, putting thumbs up, putting thumbs down, pointing, raising a fist, throwing hands up in the air, and using fingers to indicate a number are all examples of symbols used in organizations.

Organizational example

Cindy works for a bank and needs to give a presentation to a group of potential customers on the benefits of an Individual Retirement Account (IRA). She uses PowerPoint along with a prepared speech, and the customers appear to be very receptive. As she leaves the meeting, her boss gives her a "thumbs up" to signify that she did a good job.

Cindy's boss used a symbol to indicate that she did a good job.

Facial expressions

Facial expressions are a very common and important aspect of non-verbal communication because the face is the first thing people see. Typically, the face is seen before any words are spoken, and it indicates what is about to transpire. Laughing, crying, frowning, wincing, winking, and staring are all examples of facial expressions used in organizations.

Organizational example

Chester owns an automotive repair shop. When his office manager comes back from lunch, she is crying. Without any words spoken, Chester knows that something is upsetting her. It turns out that she just found out her father has terminal cancer.

The office manager's facial expression indicated that she was sad before any words were spoken.

Paralanguage

As noted in the introduction of this book, some components of speech are part of non-verbal communication. These components are known as paralanguage, and they include voice quality, speed, pitch, tone, and volume. Paralanguage is common in organizations when employees want to emphasize their points or positions.

Organizational example

Penelope works as a prison guard. If fighting occurs among inmates, she raises her voice and yells commands for everyone to be silent and sit on the ground. This accentuates her position that all prisoners need to submit until the area is restored to an orderly manner.

Paralanguage helps Penelope communicate more forcefully in chaotic situations.

Body position

Body position is people's posture, stance, or pose while interacting with others. It can indicate a variety of feelings including anger, pride, embarrassment, guilt, defensiveness, and shame. Arm crossing, leg crossing, lowering head, raising head, slouching, and chest protrusion are examples of body language used in organizations.

Organizational example

Brett works in the meat department at a grocery store. He is in charge of stocking product shelves for customers, and he takes pride in his work.

This is a very busy time for the store. Thanksgiving is next week, and Brett knows that the meat department sales will be very high until the holiday. He finishes stocking the shelves and is satisfied with his work.

A little later in the day, Brett is in the cooler taking inventory when he is paged into the meat department by his manager Erin. In a friendly tone, Erin asks him if he stocked all the necessary meat items. Brett looks at the shelves and immediately realizes he forgot to stock turkeys. He lowers his head and slumps his shoulders because he feels embarrassed that he overlooked the most important item of the holiday.

Brett's feelings were revealed in his body position.

Space position

This is the amount of space people keep between themselves and others. It is dictated by a variety of factors including situation, culture, social norms, and people's personalities. Getting close to people, keeping distance from people, and walking away from people are examples of space positions used in organizations.

Organizational example

Maxine is a dental hygienist for a dental practice. Dr. Pakrately is one of the dentists at the practice, and he makes Maxine uncomfortable during face-to-face communication. He gets very close to her during conversations, and this makes her feel like he is invading her personal space.

Dr. Pakrately's space position during personal conversation creates discomfort for Maxine because she feels he gets too close to her.

Exterior presentation

Exterior presentation essentially involves developing an image based on the way people look, the items they wear, or the things they have on their bodies. Clothing, jewelry, tattoos, uniforms, hats, and hairstyle are examples of exterior presentation used in organizations.

Interestingly, the intent of this non-verbal communication can go from one extreme to the other. Some people want to personalize their appearance, while others want to show they are part of a group. Let's examine these two extremes in more detail.

Personal intent

This kind of exterior presentation occurs when people want to establish their identity as individuals in an organization.

Organizational example

Teddy is a 43-year-old blueprint designer for a commercial builder, and he also works part-time as a rock guitarist. Most men in their 40's have short hair, but Teddy lets his hair grow past his shoulders because he views long hair as an important aspect of being a musician.

Teddy's exterior presentation establishes his individual identity at the commercial builder.

Group intent

This kind of exterior presentation occurs when people want to establish their identity as part of an organization.

Organizational example

Suzie is a delivery person for a pizza company. She wears a company hat and shirt whenever she delivers product to customers. She likes the fact that people recognize her and know why she is coming to their door.

Suzie's exterior presentation establishes her identity as part of the pizza company.

Physical touch

Also known as haptics, this occurs when people touch each other during interaction. Similar to space position, it is also affected by a variety of factors including situation, culture, social norms, and people's personalities. Pats on the back, high-fives, and handshakes are all examples of physical touch used in organizations.

Organizational example

Kenny and Ray are police officers. They are working on a case involving a known drug dealer, and they need a search warrant to gather evidence from a home and make an arrest.

A judge decides to grant the officers a search warrant after she reads the information they have submitted to her. This makes Kenny and Ray happy, and they high-five each other after being told the decision.

Kenny and Ray's high-five establishes their delight about receiving good news.

Combination

Different types of non-verbal communication can be combined to produce an even more intensified effect. This is beneficial in many workplace situations.

Organizational example

Jack and Jenny own a kitchen design company, and a customer needs 22 kitchens remodeled in an apartment complex. This job, however, is challenging because the cost is a major factor.

Jenny has spent the past week designing three different kitchens that she thinks will work. However, when Jack crunches the numbers, all of the designs exceed the cost requirement. Jack tells Jenny that she needs to quickly design something less expensive because the customer wants to get started as soon as possible.

Jenny goes back to the drawing board and comes up with two new ideas. Jack figures the costs on these designs and again finds that both are too expensive for the project. Now Jack is feeling pressure. He tells Jenny that her ideas are again too costly, and she needs to change her thinking. Jenny becomes defensive and says she is doing her best. Frustrated, Jack throws his arms up in the air (symbol), frowns (facial expression), and walks away (space position).

Jack's frustration was vividly expressed using a symbol, facial expression, and space position.

You are now aware of several different types of organizational communication that allow people to exchange information without using the spoken or written word. Non-verbal communication is advantageous in many different situations, but it is not foolproof or without issues. Since the challenges involved are important for a complete understanding of non-verbal communication, they will be discussed in the next section.

Challenges

There is little doubt that non-verbal communication in organizations can be misunderstood. This misunderstanding results from cultural differences, individual perceptions, false assumptions, physical disabilities, and a variety of other factors. In short, barriers exist when people communicate non-verbally in workplaces.

Let's look at some limitations of non-verbal communication and examples of their application in organizations.

Multi-tasking

Many times non-verbal communication requires the receiver to recognize a few different actions to understand the meaning of the message being sent. For instance, a raised fist might have a different meaning depending on whether the sender is smiling or frowning, and multi-tasking is required on the part of the receiver to notice both the symbolic gesture and the facial expression.

Organizational example

Lisa and Andy work in a restaurant at a mall food court. They share a cooler with another restaurant, and lately, the other restaurant has been using more than their half of the cooler space. Lisa needs to fit ten boxes of eggs in the cooler, but there Is only room for five, so she stacks them on top of each other. Andy sees this and becomes upset because he knows the boxes might collapse and some of the eggs could break. He frowns, shakes his head, points at the other restaurant, and storms off.   During Andy's aggressive display of non-verbal communication, Lisa does not see him point at the other restaurant. All she sees is his frown, head shake, and stormy exit.   She believes he is mad at her because she made a mistake by double stacking the eggs, but this is actually not the case. Andy is mad at the employees of the other restaurant for taking up more than their fair share of space, and he points at them to indicate his anger.

Andy is mad at the other restaurant, but Lisa is unable to comprehend all of his non-verbal actions for complete understanding so she misinterprets his intended message.

Cultural specifics

Some non-verbal actions, such as a smile or a frown, are universal. However, other actions, such as a "thumbs up" in the United States, are specific to cultures. If an action is specific to a culture, there is a high likelihood that it will not be understood by people in different cultures. This can cause problems for organizations that operate globally.

Organizational example

Donald is a salesperson at a company that sells wood products internationally. He attends a business meeting in Japan with a Japanese executive from a wood distribution company. At the start of the meeting, the executive hands Donald his business card. Donald puts the card in his shirt pocket. Without realizing it, Donald insulted the Japanese executive because Japanese businesspeople place high importance on business cards. The cards are to be treated with respect, and part of that respect means carrying them in a proper case. Disrespecting the card is seen as disrespecting the person whose name is on it.

Donald's non-verbal actions were unintentionally offensive due to cultural misunderstanding.

Limited explanation

This is a difficult one because non-verbal communication that is confusing cannot be further explained. If something is not understood in verbal or written communication, it can be clarified with more detailed verbal or written discussion. Non-verbal actions simply do not have this luxury.

Organizational example

Erica works for a biological research laboratory. She needs permission to access a password-protected database to get the information she needs to complete a project for a customer. She goes to her supervisor's office and asks him if she can have permission to access the database. Her supervisor looks at her, and then he walks out of his office.

Erica is confused. Her supervisor simply left his office, so she is not sure if she is going to get the permission she needs. In reality, her supervisor was going to get her a password from an IT person, but his non-verbal actions did not communicate this properly.

The supervisor's non-verbal actions did not communicate his intentions, and a lack of further explanation confused Erica.

Perception differences

People do not always see things the same way, and non-verbal behavior can be interpreted differently based on individual perception. Perception differences in workplaces can prevent tasks from being completed and hinder people from accomplishing organizational goals.

Organizational example

Ulysses is a painter at a house renovation company, and he just received a small pay raise from his boss Hillary. When she informs him of his raise, he nods his head, smiles politely, and goes back to work. Hillary believes Ulysses is happy with his pay raise based on his non-verbal actions. Ulysses' coworker Lenny, however, does not perceive his reaction the same. Lenny believes Ulysses nodded his head, smiled politely, and went back to work because he was disappointed that he did not receive a bigger raise. If the raise had been bigger, Ulysses' reaction would have been more enthusiastic.

This difference in perception could affect the house renovation company. If Hillary read Ulysses' non-verbal actions correctly, then Ulysses will be motivated to work harder. However, if Lenny's perception was correct, they Ulysses will be demotivated and might start looking for another job.

Psychological issues

When people are in a bad mood, their ability to effectively convey non-verbal actions is affected. This can create confusion in organizations as employees attempt to decipher the meaning of the message.

Organizational example

Milton works at an insurance agency. He is going through a divorce and battling depression due to the associated problems. Today he has good news for a longtime customer named Janice. Her car insurance is being reduced by 25 percent due to her excellent driving record. When Janice comes to the office, Milton tells her the good news with a frown on his face because he is personally not happy. Janice if left wondering if this really is good news and if something else is wrong.

Milton's presentation of good news with a frown on his face was confusing for Janice and caused her to search for the real meaning of his message.

Physical barriers

Non-verbal communication can be misunderstood if a person's behavior is distorted or blocked. This can cause many problems as employees try to understand each other's actions and perform their jobs effectively.

Organizational example

Claudia is a tool room clerk at an electrical supply company. Steve, an electrician, needs a specific type of copper wire for a project. He asks Claudia if she has any of this wire in stock, and she points to it. However, the stock room is cluttered with many different types of wire, and Steve thinks she is pointing wire that he does not need. He assumes the supply company is out of stock and tells his boss that he cannot complete the project because he does not have the proper wire.

Claudia's non-verbal action was distorted due to the clutter of the stock room, so Steve did not get the supplies he needed. He was prevented from doing his because of a physical barrier.

Non-verbal communication in organizations will likely always present certain challenges. However, some of these issues can be prevented using the ideas found in the next section.

Improving

It is rather obvious that non-verbal communication has a major effect on workplaces. Misinterpreted non-verbal actions create problems that are often difficult to resolve. That being said, there needs to be ways to improve employee's non-verbal communication.

Consider the following techniques for making non-verbal communication better in organizations:

Symbols

These intentional gestures, movements, and motions by employees signify the intent of the message and encourage reactions from receivers. They can be improved by increasing enthusiasm, and this is be accomplished by combining other non-verbal types of communication such as smiling, frowning, or shaking hands.

Organizational example

Tonya manages a team of four microbiology laboratory technicians that have been working on a cost reduction project for the lab. Today they presented their findings to the CEO, and she was very pleased. She immediately made plans to implement four of their five ideas and tells the team she wants them to work together in the future.

Tonya is very happy that the presentation went well. She meets with the team afterward and gives them a "thumbs up" for a great job. She also "high-fives" each member to make them feel a sense of accomplishment and appreciation.

Tonya combines physical touch (high-five) with a symbol (thumbs up) to strengthen her non-verbal message.

Facial Expressions

A face is typically the first part of the body seen by coworkers, so it needs to accurately reflect the message being sent. This type of non-verbal communication can be improved by becoming more aware of facial expressions to make sure that they do not conflict with the intended message.

Organizational example

Benjamin tends to smile a lot because he is typically a happy person. However, today he needs to tell two employees that their positions are being eliminated and their services with the company will no longer be needed.

Before meeting with the employees, Benjamin does a mental check of his emotions and puts on his "game face." He makes certain that he is not smiling when he meets with the employees to avoid sending unintentional messages. He wants to be serious and show compassion during this difficult time, and he does not want to appear as if he thinks any part of the situation is humorous.

Benjamin is aware of his facial expressions, and he makes sure he uses them appropriately.

Paralanguage

Paralanguage is used when employees want to accentuate their position or thinking. It includes volume, tone, and pitch of the voice, and it has some very powerful effects. For this reason, it must be recognized and altered before using it negatively.

Organizational example

Veronica is a writer for a newspaper. Her boss tells her to interview a renowned heart specialist, Dr. James Brandt, for an article on heart health. Veronica has interviewed Dr. Brandt before, and she finds him very rude and arrogant. Her natural reaction is to sigh and state how she despises this man in a very negative tone. Instead, she realizes this article will be beneficial for many readers, so she composes herself and tells her boss in a calm voice that she will get the job done.

Veronica realizes that a sigh and negative tone of voice will have detrimental effects in this situation, so she changes her paralanguage to sound more positive and professional.

Body position

Body position involves employees' stance, posture, and physical pose during face-to-face communication. In some situations, it indicates negative feelings including anger and disdain, and it needs to be modified to avoid unnecessary conflict.

Organizational example

Nadine is a salesperson at a car dealership, and she does not trust a mechanic named Hector to do honest work on her customer's vehicles. After a customer complains that his repair bill is $1200, Nadine approaches Hector to find out why the cost is so high. When she meets with Hector, her natural reaction is to cross her arms indicating disapproval. However, Nadine realizes that this body position will invite conflict, so she makes sure her arms are kept at her waist in a less threatening manner.

Nadine might not be able to get the repair bill reduced, but she understands that a defensive stance could intensify her problems with Hector, so she alters his body position.

Space position

This involves the distance people keep between themselves and others. It is often controlled by the culture or situation, so employees need to understand the specifics involved to respect the space allowed or required by coworkers, vendors, and customers.

Organizational example

Christopher works for a venture capitalist group. He is trying to convince an oil baron in Saudi Arabia to let his company invest money in new drilling equipment. Christopher realizes that the culture in Saudi Arabia allows for much closer face-to-face communication, so he is not uncomfortable when the oil baron gets very close to him during their meeting.

Christopher understands the culture in Saudi Arabia, so he allows space positioning that is much closer than that customarily found in the United States. This is the correct way to conduct business and show respect for the potential customer.

Exterior presentation

People develop images by wearing clothes, jewelry, hairstyles, hats, or body art. This is known as exterior presentation, and in organizations, it helps people personalize their appearance or show that they are part of a group.

Personal intent

This kind of exterior presentation occurs when people want to establish their identity as individuals in an organization. Employees need to be keenly aware that the way they appear communicates information about their personalities, and they should make appearance choices based on the situation.

Organizational example

Michael works at a beer distributor. Both of his arms are tattooed as "sleeves." Some of the younger employees like his body art. They comment on his drawing choices and hang out with him after work. However, certain older management employees are not as enthused with Michael's tattoos and tend to keep their distance from him. They don't understand why he would do this to his arms, and they see his body art as a sign of trouble.

Michael likes his tattoos and has no plans to remove them. If he wants to express his individualism, then he can keep them exposed. However, he can also hide them with long sleeve shirts if he wants to move into the management ranks. He has choices and needs to choose wisely based on the situation.

Group intent

This kind of exterior presentation occurs when people want to establish their identity as part of an organization. Logos, hats, and uniforms are often used to show that people are employees of an organization. Because of this, employees need to respect the company clothing their wear so it does not negatively impact the organization.

Organizational example

Brian and Karen work for a Submarine Sandwich Shop, and they are required to wear a company shirt and hat. Brian wears his hat sideways, and his shirt is always wrinkled and dirty. Customers are not comfortable with Brian preparing their sandwiches because they perceive him as unkempt and unclean. Karen, on the other hand, represents the sub company differently. She wears her hat straight and washes her uniform every night. Customers believe she is tidy and clean, and they have no objections when she prepares their food.

Brain and Karen wear the same company hat and shirt, but customers react differently based on the respect that each employee shows for the uniform.

Physical touch

This involves people touching each other during interaction. Physical touch is determined by the situation, and it can be improved in many instances. Employees need to sense when it is appropriate to use physical touch or the result could be an awkward or uncomfortable situation.

Organizational example

Charles and Alan work for a cable television news station. A reporter named Evelyn visits them at their set. Alan has known Evelyn well for over 15 years, but this is Charles' first meeting with her. Alan greets Evelyn with a hug, and it is obvious that they are longtime friends. Charles simply shakes her hand and tells her it is a pleasure to meet her.

Charles understands that he should not hug Evelyn because he has not established the same relationship that Alan has with her. A handshake is appropriate to avoid a potentially uncomfortable situation.

Summary

In organizations, actions often speak louder than words...and this is precisely why non-verbal communication is so important. This book discusses that importance by examining various types of non-verbal behavior and the challenges involved with conveying the intended messages. Also included are ways to improve non-verbal communication in organizations.

This book has an advantage over similar books because it uses real-world examples for illustration and clarification. Each section includes workplace situations that apply the concepts being discussed to simplify the understanding of non-verbal communication in organizations and make the reading more enjoyable.